PERFORMANCE ASSESSMENT TEACHER'S GUIDE

5

Printed in the U.S.A.

ISBN 978-0-544-46542-8

6 7 8 9 10   0928   23 22 21 20 19 18 17 16 15

4500533209   A B C D E F G

Approaching Performance Assessments with Confidence

By Carol Jago

The best assessments reflect best practice. Rather than asking students to perform artificial tasks, assessments worth giving include texts worth reading and tasks worth doing. Ideally, time spent on such formative assessments shouldn't be time lost to instruction but rather an opportunity both for students to demonstrate what they have learned as well as a chance for additional practice.

Malcolm Gladwell estimates in his book *Outliers* that mastering a skill requires about 10,000 hours of dedicated practice. He argues that individuals who are outstanding in their field have one thing in common—many, many hours of working at it. Gladwell claims that success is less dependent on innate talent than it is on practice. Now I'm pretty sure that I could put in 10,000 hours at a ballet studio and still be a terrible dancer, but I agree with Gladwell that, "Practice isn't the thing you do once you're good. It's the thing you do that makes you good."

Not just any kind of practice will help students master performance assessments, though. Effective practice needs to focus on improvement. That is why this series of reading and writing tasks begins with a model of the kind of reading and writing students are working towards, then takes them through practice exercises, and finally invites them to perform the skills they have practiced.

Once through the cycle is only the beginning. You will want your students to repeat the process several times over until close reading, supporting claims with evidence, and crafting a compelling essay is something they approach with confidence. Notice that I didn't say "with ease." I wish it were otherwise, but in my experience as a teacher and as an author, writing well is never easy.

I hope you find these assessment tools a valuable, seamless addition to your curriculum.

Unit 3 Response to Literature

The Way I See It

Unit 4 Narrative

Surprising Meetings

Unit 5 Mixed Practice

On Your Own

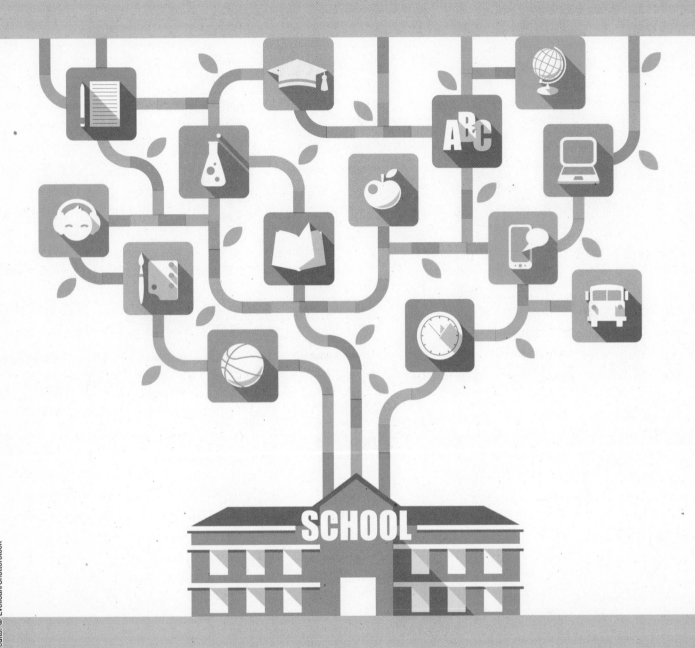

School: What Works?

STEP 1 ANALYZE THE MODEL

Do we need school libraries?

Page 5
Discuss and Decide

As students discuss what services the Holton Elementary Library will offer students, remind them to cite textual evidence.

Page 7
Discuss and Decide

As students discuss whether or not we need school libraries, remind them to cite textual evidence.

Page 9
Discuss and Decide

As students discuss whether or not they are convinced by Nahee's essay, remind them to cite textual evidence.

Page 10
Be Clear!

Accept reasonable sentences that demonstrate clarification of Nahee's ideas.

STEP 2 PRACTICE THE TASK

Is art class important?

Page 13
Discuss and Decide

As students discuss why the author thinks art classes should not be part of the school day, remind them to cite textual evidence.

Page 15
Discuss and Decide

As students discuss what the author thinks makes art different from other school subjects, remind them to cite textual evidence.

Page 17
Discuss and Decide

As students discuss one positive change that resulted from the Turnaround Arts program, remind them to cite textual evidence.

Pages 18–19

1. Accept responses that demonstrate comprehension and draw evidence from each source. The blog and the magazine article agree that art class is important, and the editorial does not agree.

2. Prose Constructed-Response

Scoring Notes: Use the rubric to evaluate student responses. Responses may include but are not limited to:

- The reasons given in the blog.

- The data and supporting details in the magazine article.

2	The response gives sufficient evidence of the ability to cite reasons that support opinions and/or ideas.
1	The response gives limited evidence of the ability to cite reasons that support opinions and/or ideas.
0	The response provides no evidence of the ability to cite reasons that support opinions and/or ideas.

3. Prose Constructed-Response

Scoring Notes: Use the rubric to evaluate student responses. Responses may include but are not limited to:

- The data and supporting details in the editorial.

2	The response gives sufficient evidence of the ability to cite reasons that support opinions and/or ideas.
1	The response gives limited evidence of the ability to cite reasons that support opinions and/or ideas.
0	The response provides no evidence of the ability to cite reasons that support opinions and/or ideas.

Pages 20–21

Planning and Prewriting

Review and critique students' planning charts; offer feedback as needed.

Scoring Notes: Use the rubric to evaluate student responses.

	Development of Ideas	Organization	Clarity of Language	Language and Conventions
4	The response addresses the prompt and shows effective and comprehensive development of the opinion using text-based evidence, clear and convincing reasoning, and/or description.	The response demonstrates coherence and clarity, a logical organization that includes an introduction and conclusion, and a logical progression of ideas.	The response establishes and maintains an effective style, including precise language, descriptive words and phrases, connecting words and phrases, and academic vocabulary.	The response demonstrates a command of standard English conventions consistent with effectively edited writing.
3	The response addresses the prompt and shows effective development of the topic using text-based evidence, reasoning, and/or description.	The response demonstrates some logical organization and includes an introduction and conclusion.	Some descriptive words, as well as some connecting words and phrases, are used to express ideas with clarity.	The response demonstrates a command of standard English conventions, although there may be some minor errors in grammar and usage.
2	The response addresses the prompt and shows some development of the topic but fails to use text-based evidence, reasoning, and/or description.	The response demonstrates little logical organization and includes either an introduction or a conclusion.	Few descriptive words, as well as a few connecting words and phrases, are used and ideas are not expressed as clearly as possible.	The response demonstrates a command of standard English conventions, although there are major errors in grammar and usage.

1	The response does not directly address the prompt, shows no development of the topic, and fails to use text-based evidence, reasoning, and/or description.	The response demonstrates little logical organization and fails to include either an introduction or a conclusion.	No descriptive words or connecting words and phrases are used and ideas are not expressed with clarity.	Errors in grammar and usage create confusion of meaning.
0	The response demonstrates no evidence of the ability to write an opinion essay.			

STEP 3 PERFORM THE TASK

How much homework should teachers assign?

Page 27
Close Read

Student answers should demonstrate comprehension and draw evidence from the text. They may cite how homework creates pressure for students, how extra work does not reward students who learn quickly, how there are many factors besides homework that impact academic performance, or how it burdens students with extra responsibility.

Page 29
Close Read

Student answers should demonstrate comprehension and draw evidence from the text. They may cite that Principal Reed supports how homework reinforces what students learn, how it improves understanding and test-taking skills, or that it shouldn't take more than an hour a day.

Page 30
Discuss and Decide

As students discuss why the percentage of students who have less than an hour of homework has increased, remind them to cite textual evidence.

Pages 31–32

1. d.

2. c.

3. d.

4. b.

5. Accept responses that demonstrate comprehension and draw evidence from the source. The newspaper editorial supports the position that there should not be any homework, and the letter to parents supports the position that there should be about an hour of homework each night. The survey results indicate a trend toward more homework.

6. Prose Constructed-Response

Scoring Notes: Use the rubric to evaluate student responses. Responses may include but are not limited to:

- Audrey's editorial is based on an interview with her teacher, Mrs. Duffy. Audrey uses phrases such as "Mrs. Duffy says" or "Mrs. Duffy told me" to signal her teacher's opinion to the reader.

- For each of her teacher's opinions, Audrey provides a counterpoint opinion. Audrey uses phrases such as "I think" or "I say" to signal her own opinion to the reader.

- Audrey's editorial is balanced. She gives her teacher's opinion and her own opinion equal weight. She shows her teacher's responses in bold, and discusses the pro and con in each paragraph.

2	The response gives sufficient evidence of the ability to cite reasons that support opinions and/or ideas.
1	The response gives limited evidence of the ability to cite reasons that support opinions and/or ideas.
0	The response provides no evidence of the ability to cite reasons that support opinions and/or ideas.

Pages 33–34
Opinion Essay

Scoring Notes: Use the rubric to evaluate student responses.

	Development of Ideas	Organization	Clarity of Language	Language and Conventions
4	The response addresses the prompt and shows effective and comprehensive development of the opinion using text-based evidence, clear and convincing reasoning, and/or description.	The response demonstrates coherence and clarity, a logical organization that includes an introduction and conclusion, and a logical progression of ideas.	The response establishes and maintains an effective style, including precise language, descriptive words and phrases, connecting words and phrases, and academic vocabulary.	The response demonstrates a command of standard English conventions consistent with effectively edited writing.
3	The response addresses the prompt and shows effective development of the topic using text-based evidence, reasoning, and/or description.	The response demonstrates some logical organization and includes an introduction and conclusion.	Some descriptive words, as well as some connecting words and phrases, are used to express ideas with clarity.	The response demonstrates a command of standard English conventions, although there may be some minor errors in grammar and usage.
2	The response addresses the prompt and shows some development of the topic but fails to use text-based evidence, reasoning, and/or description.	The response demonstrates little logical organization and includes either an introduction or a conclusion.	Few descriptive words, as well as a few connecting words and phrases, are used and ideas are not expressed as clearly as possible.	The response demonstrates a command of standard English conventions, although there are major errors in grammar and usage.

	Development of Ideas	Organization	Clarity of Language	Language and Conventions
1	The response does not directly address the prompt, shows no development of the topic, and fails to use text-based evidence, reasoning, and/or description.	The response demonstrates little logical organization and fails to include either an introduction or a conclusion.	No descriptive words or connecting words and phrases are used and ideas are not expressed with clarity.	Errors in grammar and usage create confusion of meaning.
0	The response demonstrates no evidence of the ability to write an opinion essay.			

Early American Heroes

STEP 1 ANALYZE THE MODEL

What made Ann Bailey a hero?

Page 40
Close Read

Student answers should demonstrate comprehension and draw evidence from the text. They may cite that none of the men from Fort Lee volunteered to travel; that Bailey rode without stopping; or that she refused an escort on the return trip, so as not to be slowed down.

Page 41
Discuss and Decide

As students discuss Ann Bailey's attitude toward danger, remind them to cite textual evidence.

Page 43
Discuss and Decide

As students discuss what made Ann Bailey a hero according to Dolores's essay, remind them to cite textual evidence.

Page 44
Organizing an Informative Essay

Accept reasonable examples that demonstrate understanding of Dolores's main-idea-and-details informative essay, and the logical sequencing of her details.

STEP 2 PRACTICE THE TASK

What led Tecumseh to fight?

Page 47
Discuss and Decide

As students discuss how Tecumseh resisted attempts by people from the U.S. to settle on American Indian land, remind them to cite textual evidence.

Page 49
Close Read

Student answers should demonstrate comprehension and draw evidence from the text. They may cite that Pucksinwah was mortally wounded at the Battle of Point Pleasant, and that he wanted Tecumseh to continue to defend American Indian land.

Page 51

As students discuss Tecumseh's views on owning land and how they differed from those of the U.S. government, remind them to cite textual evidence.

Pages 52–53

Respond to Questions

1. b.

2. c.

3. d.

4. d.

5. Prose Constructed-Response

Scoring Notes: Use the rubric to evaluate student responses. Responses may include but are not limited to:

- Evidence of Tecumseh's desire and ability to make strategic alliances.

- Evidence describing the Battle of Tippecanoe, where the U.S. government made war against American Indian nations.

2	The response gives sufficient evidence of the ability to cite details and evidence to support ideas.
1	The response gives limited evidence of the ability to cite details and evidence to support ideas.
0	The response provides no evidence of the ability to cite details and evidence to support ideas.

6. Prose Constructed-Response

Scoring Notes: Use the rubric to evaluate student responses. Responses may include but are not limited to:

- Evidence describing how Tecumseh's father is mortally wounded during the Battle of Point Pleasant. On his deathbed, he asks Tecumseh to never make peace with the settlers. Tecumseh and his older brother engage in attacks to resist the settlers, but are pushed farther and farther west.

- Evidence describing how Tecumseh refuses to sign the Treaty of Greenville, and how he spends the next twenty years forming alliances with other American Indian nations—and even the British—to prevent the U.S. government from taking land.

- Evidence describing how Tecumseh makes an appeal to General William Henry Harrison, but his appeal is ignored. Later, Tecumseh clashes with him at the Battle of the Thames and is killed.

2	The response gives sufficient evidence of the ability to cite details and evidence to support opinions and/or ideas.
1	The response gives limited evidence of the ability to cite details and evidence to support opinions and/or ideas.
0	The response provides no evidence of the ability to cite details and evidence to support ideas.

Pages 54–55
Planning and Prewriting

Review and critique students' planning charts; offer feedback as needed.

Pages 56–58
Informative Essay

Scoring Notes: Use the rubric to evaluate student responses.

	Development of Ideas	Organization	Clarity of Language	Language and Conventions
4	The response addresses the prompt and shows effective and comprehensive development of the controlling idea using text-based evidence, clear and convincing reasoning, and/or description.	The response demonstrates coherence and clarity, a logical organization that includes an introduction and conclusion, and a logical progression of ideas.	The response establishes and maintains an effective style, including precise language, descriptive words and phrases, connecting words and phrases, and academic vocabulary.	The response demonstrates a command of standard English conventions consistent with effectively edited writing.

	Development of Ideas	Organization	Clarity of Language	Language and Conventions
3	The response addresses the prompt and shows effective development of the topic using text-based evidence, reasoning, and/or description.	The response demonstrates some logical organization and includes an introduction and conclusion.	Some descriptive words, as well as some connecting words and phrases, are used to express ideas with clarity.	The response demonstrates a command of standard English conventions, although there may be some minor errors in grammar and usage.
2	The response addresses the prompt and shows some development of the topic but fails to use text-based evidence, reasoning, and/or description.	The response demonstrates little logical organization and includes either an introduction or a conclusion.	Few descriptive words, as well as a few connecting words and phrases, are used and ideas are not expressed as clearly as possible.	The response demonstrates a command of standard English conventions, although there are major errors in grammar and usage.
1	The response does not directly address the prompt, shows no development of the topic, and fails to use text-based evidence, reasoning, and/or description.	The response demonstrates little logical organization and fails to include either an introduction or a conclusion.	No descriptive words or connecting words and phrases are used and ideas are not expressed with clarity.	Errors in grammar and usage create confusion of meaning.
0	The response demonstrates no evidence of the ability to write an informative essay.			

STEP 3 PERFORM THE TASK

How did York's life change after his adventure?

Page 61
Discuss and Decide

As students discuss details from the text and map that convey the difficulty of Lewis and Clark's journey, remind them to cite evidence.

Page 63
Close Read

Student answers should demonstrate comprehension and draw evidence from the text. They may explain that York had skills that differentiated him from others on the expedition—such as his ability to swim and care for those who were ailing. York was the first African American to cross the United States, and he also was allowed to carry a gun and vote.

Page 64
Discuss and Decide

As students discuss how York was treated differently from other members of the expedition, remind them to cite textual evidence.

Pages 65–66
Respond to Questions

1. a.

2. a.

3. b.

4. a.

5. Prose Constructed-Response

Scoring Notes: Use the rubric to evaluate student responses. Responses may include but are not limited to:

- Evidence of York's skills—his ability to gather food, cook, swim, hunt, and care for those who were ailing.

- Evidence of York's trustworthiness, which earned him the privilege to carry a gun.

- Evidence of York's courage and strength, which earned him the distinction of being the first African American to cross the U.S.

- Evidence of York's importance to the group—which earned him the distinction of being the first African American to vote.

2	The response gives sufficient evidence of the ability to cite details and evidence to support ideas.
1	The response gives limited evidence of the ability to cite details and evidence to support ideas.
0	The response provides no evidence of the ability to cite details and evidence to support ideas.

6. Prose Constructed-Response

Scoring Notes: Use the rubric to evaluate student responses. Responses may include but are not limited to:

- Evidence from the map in Source 1 that shows the length of the journey and the types of terrain the group encountered. Source 1 would indicate how challenging the going must have been for York.

- Evidence from Source 2 that shows York's day-to-day experiences, and how he interacted with others.

2	The response gives sufficient evidence of the ability to cite details and evidence to support ideas.
1	The response gives limited evidence of the ability to cite details and evidence to support ideas.
0	The response provides no evidence of the ability to cite details and evidence to support ideas.

Pages 67–68
Informative Essay

Scoring Notes: Use the rubric to evaluate student responses.

	Development of Ideas	Organization	Clarity of Language	Language and Conventions
4	The response addresses the prompt and shows effective and comprehensive development of the controlling idea using text-based evidence, clear and convincing reasoning, and/or description.	The response demonstrates coherence and clarity, a logical organization that includes an introduction and conclusion, and a logical progression of ideas.	The response establishes and maintains an effective style, including precise language, descriptive words and phrases, connecting words and phrases, and academic vocabulary.	The response demonstrates a command of standard English conventions consistent with effectively edited writing.

	Development of Ideas	Organization	Clarity of Language	Language and Conventions
3	The response addresses the prompt and shows effective development of the topic using text-based evidence, reasoning, and/or description.	The response demonstrates some logical organization and includes an introduction and conclusion.	Some descriptive words, as well as some connecting words and phrases, are used to express ideas with clarity.	The response demonstrates a command of standard English conventions, although there may be some minor errors in grammar and usage.
2	The response addresses the prompt and shows some development of the topic but fails to use text-based evidence, reasoning, and/or description.	The response demonstrates little logical organization and includes either an introduction or a conclusion.	Few descriptive words, as well as a few connecting words and phrases, are used and ideas are not expressed as clearly as possible.	The response demonstrates a command of standard English conventions, although there are major errors in grammar and usage.
1	The response does not directly address the prompt, shows no development of the topic, and fails to use text-based evidence, reasoning, and/or description.	The response demonstrates little logical organization and fails to include either an introduction or a conclusion.	No descriptive words or connecting words and phrases are used and ideas are not expressed with clarity.	Errors in grammar and usage create confusion of meaning.
0	The response demonstrates no evidence of the ability to write an informative essay.			

The Way I See It

STEP 1 ANALYZE THE MODEL

How do characters interact in a story?

Page 73
Discuss and Decide

As students discuss which actions tell them that the March Hare is argumentative, remind them to cite textual evidence.

Page 75
Discuss and Decide

As students discuss the ways in which the behavior of the March Hare and the Hatter are similar, remind them to cite textual evidence.

Page 77
Discuss and Decide

As students discuss why Alice tries to stop interrupting the Dormouse, remind them to cite textual evidence.

Page 79
Close Read

Student answers should demonstrate comprehension and draw evidence from the text. They may cite how Alice continues to speak in an "offended tone" throughout the tea-party, then how the Hatter's rudeness became "more than Alice could bear." Alice walks off without anyone taking notice, and although she was "half hoping that they would call after her," they did not.

Page 81
Discuss and Decide

As students discuss Guy's main idea in his response to "A Mad Tea-Party," and how he supports his main idea with examples from the text, remind them to cite textual evidence.

Page 82
Responding to Literature

Accept reasonable responses that demonstrate understanding of the story's events, specifically of a misunderstanding between Alice and another character.

STEP 2 PRACTICE THE TASK

How does point of view influence the way events are described?

Page 85
Discuss and Decide

As students discuss how they think a human being would describe the "forest," remind them to cite textual evidence.

Page 87
Close Read

Student answers should demonstrate comprehension and draw evidence from the text. They may cite evidence that the "glassy, curved wall" is a sugar bowl, because from the "top of the wall" the ants look down "to a sea of crystals." They then climb down into the bowl to find their "sparkling treasure," sugar. Students may also cite evidence from the image beside the paragraph, which shows a sugar bowl and the ants carrying sugar crystals.

Page 89
Discuss and Decide

As students discuss the reactions the ants have to their experiences in the new surroundings, remind them to cite textual evidence.

Page 91
Discuss and Decide

As students discuss why the ants are happy to be home, remind them to cite textual evidence.

Pages 92–93
Respond to Questions

1. b.

2. a.

3. c.

4. Prose Constructed-Response

Scoring Notes: Use the rubric to evaluate student responses. Responses may include but are not limited to:

- Evidence that the ants found a hiding place in a "huge round disk with holes" (an English muffin).

- Evidence that the English muffin in which they were hiding was "lifted, tilted, and lowered into a dark space" (a toaster).

- Evidence that "they were surrounded by a strange red glow" and that it "became so unbearably hot" (the toaster heated up).
- Evidence that "the disk they were standing on rocketed upward" and the ants "went flying through the air" (the English muffin popped up, taking the ants with it).

2	The response gives sufficient evidence of the ability to gather, analyze, and integrate information within a source.
1	The response gives limited evidence of the ability to gather, analyze, and integrate information within a source.
0	The response provides no evidence of the ability to gather, analyze, and integrate information within a source.

5. Prose Constructed-Response

Scoring Notes: Use the rubric to evaluate student responses. Responses may include but are not limited to:

- Evidence that the ants think they are safe: the two narrow holes remind the ants of the "warmth and safety of their old underground home."
- Evidence that the ants had crawled into an electrical outlet: "there was no safety inside these holes," and as a "strange force passed through the wet ants" they were "stunned senseless" and "blown out of the holes."

2	The response gives sufficient evidence of the ability to gather, analyze, and integrate information within a source.
1	The response gives limited evidence of the ability to gather, analyze, and integrate information within a source.
0	The response provides no evidence of the ability to gather, analyze, and integrate information within a source.

6. Prose Constructed-Response

Scoring Notes: Use the rubric to evaluate student responses. Responses may include but are not limited to:

- Evidence that humans would see the "mountain" as a house.
- Evidence that humans would see the "ledge" as a windowsill.

2	The response gives sufficient evidence of the ability to gather, analyze, and integrate information within a source.			
1	The response gives limited evidence of the ability to gather, analyze, and integrate information within a source.			
0	The response provides no evidence of the ability to gather, analyze, and integrate information within a source.			

Pages 94–95
Planning and Prewriting

Review and critique students' planning documents; offer feedback as needed.

Pages 96–98
Response to Literature

Scoring Notes: Use the rubric to evaluate student responses.

	Development of Ideas	Organization	Clarity of Language	Language and Conventions
4	The response addresses the prompt and shows effective and comprehensive development of the controlling idea using text-based evidence, clear and convincing reasoning, and/or description.	The response demonstrates coherence and clarity, a logical organization that includes an introduction and conclusion, and a logical progression of ideas.	The response establishes and maintains an effective style, including precise language, descriptive words and phrases, connecting words and phrases, and academic vocabulary.	The response demonstrates a command of standard English conventions consistent with effectively edited writing.
3	The response addresses the prompt and shows effective development of the topic using text-based evidence, reasoning, and/or description.	The response demonstrates some logical organization and includes an introduction and conclusion.	Some descriptive words, as well as some connecting words and phrases, are used to express ideas with clarity.	The response demonstrates a command of standard English conventions, although there may be some minor errors in grammar and usage.

	Development of Ideas	Organization	Clarity of Language	Language and Conventions
2	The response addresses the prompt and shows some development of the topic but fails to use text-based evidence, reasoning, and/or description.	The response demonstrates little logical organization and includes either an introduction or a conclusion.	Few descriptive words, as well as a few connecting words and phrases, are used and ideas are not expressed as clearly as possible.	The response demonstrates a command of standard English conventions, although there are major errors in grammar and usage.
1	The response does not directly address the prompt, shows no development of the topic, and fails to use text-based evidence, reasoning, and/or description.	The response demonstrates little logical organization and fails to include either an introduction or a conclusion.	No descriptive words or connecting words and phrases are used and ideas are not expressed with clarity.	Errors in grammar and usage create confusion of meaning.
0	The response demonstrates no evidence of the ability to write a response to literature.			

STEP 3 PERFORM THE TASK

How can a narrator shape the way events are presented?

Page 101

Discuss and Decide

As students discuss whether the wolf thinks he has done something wrong, remind them to cite textual evidence.

Page 103

Discuss and Decide

As students discuss what the wolf says about why he ate the First Little Pig, remind them to cite textual evidence.

Page 105

Close Read

Student answers should demonstrate comprehension and draw evidence from the text. They may cite that the wolf thinks the Third Little Pig is "rude" and "impolite" and says bad things about the wolf's granny, which makes the wolf "go a little crazy."

1. a.

2. c.

3. b.

4. b.

5. Prose Constructed-Response

Scoring Notes: Use the rubric to evaluate student responses. Responses may include but are not limited to:

- Evidence that a pig would think the wolf is big and bad.

- Evidence that the wolf blew the pigs' houses down on purpose.

- Evidence that a pig would think the wolf just wanted to eat the Three Little Pigs.

2	The response gives sufficient evidence of the ability to gather, analyze, and integrate information within a source.
1	The response gives limited evidence of the ability to gather, analyze, and integrate information within a source.
0	The response provides no evidence of the ability to gather, analyze, and integrate information within a source.

6. Prose Constructed-Response

Scoring Notes: Use the rubric to evaluate student responses. Responses may include but are not limited to:

- Evidence that the wolf was baking a cake for his granny and needed to borrow a cup of sugar from his neighbors.

- Evidence that the Three Little Pigs were the wolf's closest neighbors.

- Evidence that the wolf had a bad sneezing cold.

- Evidence that two of the pigs' houses were badly constructed.

- Evidence that we have sympathy for the pigs because they are cute.

- Evidence that the wolf was framed.

2	The response gives sufficient evidence of the ability to gather, analyze, and integrate information within a source.
1	The response gives limited evidence of the ability to gather, analyze, and integrate information within a source.
0	The response provides no evidence of the ability to gather, analyze, and integrate information within a source.

7. Prose Constructed-Response

Scoring Notes: Use the rubric to evaluate student responses. Responses may include but are not limited to:

• Evidence that the wolf is a trustworthy narrator.

• Evidence that the wolf is not a trustworthy narrator.

2	The response gives sufficient evidence of the ability to gather, analyze, and integrate information within a source.
1	The response gives limited evidence of the ability to gather, analyze, and integrate information within a source.
0	The response provides no evidence of the ability to gather, analyze, and integrate information within a source.

Pages 109–110
Response to Literature

Scoring Notes: Use the rubric to evaluate student responses.

	Development of Ideas	Organization	Clarity of Language	Language and Conventions
4	The response addresses the prompt and shows effective and comprehensive development of the controlling idea using text-based evidence, clear and convincing reasoning, and/or description.	The response demonstrates coherence and clarity, a logical organization that includes an introduction and conclusion, and a logical progression of ideas.	The response establishes and maintains an effective style, including precise language, descriptive words and phrases, connecting words and phrases, and academic vocabulary.	The response demonstrates a command of standard English conventions consistent with effectively edited writing.

	Development of Ideas	Organization	Clarity of Language	Language and Conventions
3	The response addresses the prompt and shows effective development of the topic using text-based evidence, reasoning, and/or description.	The response demonstrates some logical organization and includes an introduction and conclusion.	Some descriptive words, as well as some connecting words and phrases, are used to express ideas with clarity.	The response demonstrates a command of standard English conventions, although there may be some minor errors in grammar and usage.
2	The response addresses the prompt and shows some development of the topic but fails to use text-based evidence, reasoning, and/or description.	The response demonstrates little logical organization and includes either an introduction or a conclusion.	Few descriptive words, as well as a few connecting words and phrases, are used and ideas are not expressed as clearly as possible.	The response demonstrates a command of standard English conventions, although there are major errors in grammar and usage.
1	The response does not directly address the prompt, shows no development of the topic, and fails to use text-based evidence, reasoning, and/or description.	The response demonstrates little logical organization and fails to include either an introduction or a conclusion.	No descriptive words or connecting words and phrases are used and ideas are not expressed with clarity.	Errors in grammar and usage create confusion of meaning.
0	The response demonstrates no evidence of the ability to write a response to literature.			

Surprising Meetings

STEP 1 ANALYZE THE MODEL

What happens when Houdini meets Einstein?

Page 117

Close Read

Student answers should demonstrate comprehension and draw evidence from the text. They may suggest that Einstein would ask Houdini questions about how his tricks worked.

Page 119

Discuss and Decide

As students discuss two factual examples from the sources that Jane used in her narrative, remind them to cite textual evidence.

Page 120

Set the Scene!

Accept reasonable sentences that demonstrate understanding of the different settings that Jane uses in her narrative, and how the development of one setting description could strengthen her narrative.

STEP 2 PRACTICE THE TASK

What happens when superheroes compete at a field day?

Page 125

Close Read

Student answers should demonstrate comprehension and draw evidence from the text. They may cite that Zip Girl's speed would help her in any of the race events.

Pages 126–127

Respond to Questions

1. a.

2. b.

3. d.

4. Prose Constructed-Response

Scoring Notes: Use the rubric to evaluate student responses. Responses may include but are not limited to:

- Evidence that Tough Guy's super strength would help him win the tug of war.

- Evidence that the Aphid Kid's extra legs would help him win the tug of war.

2	The response gives sufficient evidence of the ability to utilize factual information from multiple sources to support a narrative.
1	The response gives limited evidence of the ability to utilize factual information from multiple sources to support a narrative.
0	The response gives no evidence of the ability to support a narrative with factual information from multiple sources.

5. Prose Constructed-Response

Scoring Notes: Use the rubric to evaluate student responses. Responses may include but are not limited to:

- Evidence that Tough Guy might be too strong for certain events—he might break the rope in the tug of war, or the bar in the pull-up contest.

- Evidence that Zip Girl might run too fast to pass the baton in the relay race.

- Evidence that the Aphid Kid cannot enter the three-legged race because he has six legs—and might focus on eating plants and grass instead of participating in the field day events.

2	The response gives sufficient evidence of the ability to utilize factual information from multiple sources to support a narrative.
1	The response gives limited evidence of the ability to utilize factual information from multiple sources to support a narrative.
0	The response gives no evidence of the ability to support a narrative with factual information from multiple sources.

© Houghton Mifflin Harcourt Publishing Company

6. Prose Constructed-Response

Scoring Notes: Use the rubric to evaluate student responses. Responses may include but are not limited to:

- Evidence that Tough Guy's strength and the Aphid Kid's extra legs would win the tug of war.

- Evidence that Zip Girl's speed and Tough Guy's endurance would win the relay race.

- Evidence that Zip Girl's speed and the Aphid Kid's extra legs would win the three-legged race.

2	The response gives sufficient evidence of the ability to utilize factual information from multiple sources to support a narrative.
1	The response gives limited evidence of the ability to utilize factual information from multiple sources to support a narrative.
0	The response gives no evidence of the ability to support a narrative with factual information from multiple sources.

Pages 128–129
Planning and Prewriting

Review and critique students' planning documents; offer feedback as needed.

Pages 130–132
Narrative

Scoring Notes: Use the rubric to evaluate student responses.

	Development of Ideas	Organization	Clarity of Language	Language and Conventions
4	The response addresses the prompt and effectively establishes a narrator, setting, and characters.	The response demonstrates coherence and clarity, a logical organization that includes an introduction and conclusion, and a logical progression of ideas.	The response establishes and maintains an effective style, including precise language, descriptive words and phrases, connecting words and phrases, and dialogue.	The response demonstrates a command of standard English conventions consistent with effectively edited writing.

	Development of Ideas	Organization	Clarity of Language	Language and Conventions
3	The response addresses the prompt and adequately establishes a narrator, setting, and characters.	The response demonstrates some logical organization and includes an introduction and conclusion.	Some descriptive words, as well as some connecting words and phrases, are used to express ideas with clarity.	The response demonstrates a command of standard English conventions, although there may be some minor errors in grammar and usage.
2	The response addresses the prompt, but inconsistently establishes a narrator, setting, and characters.	The response demonstrates little logical organization and includes either an introduction or a conclusion.	Few descriptive words and few connecting words and phrases are used, and ideas are not expressed as clearly as possible.	The response demonstrates a command of standard English conventions, although there are major errors in grammar and usage.
1	The response does not directly address the prompt, and does not establish a narrator, setting, or characters.	The response demonstrates little logical organization and fails to include either an introduction or a conclusion.	No descriptive words or connecting words or phrases are used, and ideas are not expressed with clarity.	Errors in grammar and usage create confusion of meaning.
0	The response demonstrates no evidence of the ability to write a narrative.			

STEP 3 PERFORM THE TASK

What happens when you realize you are not alone in a strange house?

Page 135
Close Read

Student answers should demonstrate comprehension and draw evidence from the text. They may cite that Mr. Smith would have books on Venus fly traps, antique suits of armor, and mummies—among his books on Rube Goldberg machines.

Pages 137–138

1. b.

2. b.

3. c.

4. a.

5. Prose Constructed-Response

Scoring Notes: Use the rubric to evaluate student responses. Responses may include but are not limited to:

- Evidence that Mr. Smith shows two suits of armor in the Grand Hallway.

- Evidence describing the suits of armor: that they are huge, heavy, and very old.

2	The response gives sufficient evidence of the ability to utilize factual information from multiple sources to support a narrative.
1	The response gives limited evidence of the ability to utilize factual information from multiple sources to support a narrative.
0	The response gives no evidence of the ability to support a narrative with factual information from multiple sources.

6. Prose Constructed-Response

Scoring Notes: Use the rubric to evaluate student responses. Responses may include but are not limited to:

- Evidence that Mr. Smith's house has large rooms, each devoted to one of his collections.

- Evidence that the Grand Hallway opens on to each collection, except the T-Rex skeleton.

- Evidence that the Secret Underground Passageway would allow someone to get from the front of the house to the back of the house without being seen.

2	The response gives sufficient evidence of the ability to utilize factual information from multiple sources to support a narrative.
1	The response gives limited evidence of the ability to utilize factual information from multiple sources to support a narrative.
0	The response gives no evidence of the ability to support a narrative with factual information from multiple sources.

7. Prose Constructed-Response

Scoring Notes: Use the rubric to evaluate student responses. Responses may include but are not limited to:

- Evidence that someone could hide in the secret underground passageway because people who had never visited wouldn't know it was there.

- Evidence that someone could hide behind the mummies, T-Rex skeleton, or the suits of armor, because they are all large.

2	The response gives sufficient evidence of the ability to utilize factual information from multiple sources to support a narrative.
1	The response gives limited evidence of the ability to utilize factual information from multiple sources to support a narrative.
0	The response gives no evidence of the ability to support a narrative with factual information from multiple sources.

Pages 139–140
Narrative Essay

Scoring Notes: Use the rubric to evaluate student responses.

	Development of Ideas	Organization	Clarity of Language	Language and Conventions
4	The response addresses the prompt and effectively establishes a narrator, setting, and characters.	The response demonstrates coherence and clarity, a logical organization that includes an introduction and conclusion, and a logical progression of ideas.	The response establishes and maintains an effective style, including precise language, descriptive words and phrases, connecting words and phrases, and dialogue.	The response demonstrates a command of standard English conventions consistent with effectively edited writing.

	Development of Ideas	Organization	Clarity of Language	Language and Conventions
3	The response addresses the prompt and adequately establishes a narrator, setting, and characters.	The response demonstrates some logical organization and includes an introduction and conclusion.	Some descriptive words, as well as some connecting words and phrases, are used to express ideas with clarity.	The response demonstrates a command of standard English conventions, although there may be some minor errors in grammar and usage.
2	The response addresses the prompt, but inconsistently establishes a narrator, setting, and characters.	The response demonstrates little logical organization and includes either an introduction or a conclusion.	Few descriptive words and few connecting words and phrases are used, and ideas are not expressed as clearly as possible.	The response demonstrates a command of standard English conventions, although there are major errors in grammar and usage.
1	The response does not directly address the prompt, and does not establish a narrator, setting, or characters.	The response demonstrates little logical organization and fails to include either an introduction or a conclusion.	No descriptive words or connecting words or phrases are used, and ideas are not expressed with clarity.	Errors in grammar and usage create confusion of meaning.
0	The response demonstrates no evidence of the ability to write a narrative.			

On Your Own

TASK 1 OPINION ESSAY

Page 151

1. d.

2. Prose Constructed-Response

Scoring Notes: Use the rubric to evaluate student responses. Responses may include but are not limited to:

- Evidence that summer months are a time for relaxation and fun, not assignments.

- Evidence that required reading takes the fun out of reading for enjoyment.

- Evidence that assigned reading discourages a love of reading by making it a chore or a source of tension.

2	The response gives sufficient evidence of the ability to cite reasons that support opinions and/or ideas.
1	The response gives limited evidence of the ability to cite reasons that support opinions and/or ideas.
0	The response gives no evidence of the ability to cite reasons that support opinions and/or ideas.

3. Prose Constructed-Response

Scoring Notes: Use the rubric to evaluate student responses. Responses may include but are not limited to:

- Evidence that students should feel less pressure to read over the summer, since they do not have their regularly assigned homework.

- Evidence that reading is fun, and students can find out what interests them.

- Evidence that summer reading is portable; audio books and mp3s make it easy and enjoyable to listen to books while doing other things.

- Evidence that students have a variety of interesting books to choose from.

2	The response gives sufficient evidence of the ability to cite reasons that support opinions and/or ideas.
1	The response gives limited evidence of the ability to cite reasons that support opinions and/or ideas.
0	The response provides no evidence of the ability to cite reasons that support opinions and/or ideas.

Page 152
Opinion Essay

Scoring Notes: Use the rubric to evaluate student responses.

	Development of Ideas	Organization	Clarity of Language	Language and Conventions
4	The response addresses the prompt and shows effective and comprehensive development of the opinion using text-based evidence, clear and convincing reasoning, and/or description.	The response demonstrates coherence and clarity, a logical organization that includes an introduction and conclusion, and a logical progression of ideas.	The response establishes and maintains an effective style, including precise language, descriptive words and phrases, connecting words and phrases, and academic vocabulary.	The response demonstrates a command of standard English conventions consistent with effectively edited writing.
3	The response addresses the prompt and shows effective development of the topic using text-based evidence, reasoning, and/or description.	The response demonstrates some logical organization and includes an introduction and conclusion.	Some descriptive words, as well as some connecting words and phrases, are used to express ideas with clarity.	The response demonstrates a command of standard English conventions, although there may be some minor errors in grammar and usage.
2	The response addresses the prompt and shows some development of the topic but fails to use text-based evidence, reasoning, and/or description.	The response demonstrates little logical organization and includes either an introduction or a conclusion.	Few descriptive words, as well as a few connecting words and phrases, are used and ideas are not expressed as clearly as possible.	The response demonstrates a command of standard English conventions, although there are major errors in grammar and usage.

	Development of Ideas	Organization	Clarity of Language	Language and Conventions
1	The response does not directly address the prompt, shows no development of the topic, and fails to use text-based evidence, reasoning, and/or description.	The response demonstrates little logical organization and fails to include either an introduction or a conclusion.	No descriptive words or connecting words and phrases are used and ideas are not expressed with clarity.	Errors in grammar and usage create confusion of meaning.
0	The response demonstrates no evidence of the ability to write an opinion essay.			

TASK 2 INFORMATIVE ESSAY

Page 161

1. b.

2. d.

3. c.

Page 162

Informative Essay

Scoring Notes: Use the rubric to evaluate student responses.

	Development of Ideas	Organization	Clarity of Language	Language and Conventions
4	The response addresses the prompt and shows effective and comprehensive development of the controlling idea using text-based evidence, clear and convincing reasoning, and/or description.	The response demonstrates coherence and clarity, a logical organization that includes an introduction and conclusion, and a logical progression of ideas.	The response establishes and maintains an effective style, including precise language, descriptive words and phrases, connecting words and phrases, and academic vocabulary.	The response demonstrates a command of standard English conventions consistent with effectively edited writing.

	Development of Ideas	Organization	Clarity of Language	Language and Conventions
3	The response addresses the prompt and shows effective development of the topic using text-based evidence, reasoning, and/or description.	The response demonstrates some logical organization and includes an introduction and conclusion.	Some descriptive words, as well as some connecting words and phrases, are used to express ideas with clarity.	The response demonstrates a command of standard English conventions, although there may be some minor errors in grammar and usage.
2	The response addresses the prompt and shows some development of the topic but fails to use text-based evidence, reasoning, and/or description.	The response demonstrates little logical organization and includes either an introduction or a conclusion.	Few descriptive words, as well as a few connecting words and phrases, are used and ideas are not expressed as clearly as possible.	The response demonstrates a command of standard English conventions, although there are major errors in grammar and usage.
1	The response does not directly address the prompt, shows no development of the topic, and fails to use text-based evidence, reasoning, and/or description.	The response demonstrates little logical organization and fails to include either an introduction or a conclusion.	No descriptive words or connecting words and phrases are used and ideas are not expressed with clarity.	Errors in grammar and usage create confusion of meaning.
0	The response demonstrates no evidence of the ability to write an informative essay.			

TASK 3 RESPONSE TO LITERATURE

Page 171

1. d.

2. Prose Constructed-Response

Scoring Notes: Use the rubric to evaluate student responses. Responses may include but are not limited to:

- Evidence that the woodcutter saved the pheasant from being killed by the snake.

2	The response gives sufficient evidence of the ability to gather, analyze, and integrate information within a source.
1	The response gives limited evidence of the ability to gather, analyze, and integrate information within a source.
0	The response provides no evidence of the ability to gather, analyze, and integrate information within a source.

3. Prose Constructed-Response

Scoring Notes: Use the rubric to evaluate student responses. Responses may include but are not limited to:

- Evidence that the woodcutter recognized that the snake was going to kill the pheasant, and so he killed the snake to protect the pheasant.

- Evidence that the snake believed his killing by the woodcutter was unjust, and so he sought revenge.

2	The response gives sufficient evidence of the ability to gather, analyze, and integrate information within a source.
1	The response gives limited evidence of the ability to gather, analyze, and integrate information within a source.
0	The response provides no evidence of the ability to gather, analyze, and integrate information within a source.

Page 172
Response to Literature

Scoring Notes: Use the rubric to evaluate student responses.

	Development of Ideas	Organization	Clarity of Language	Language and Conventions
4	The response addresses the prompt and shows effective and comprehensive development of the controlling idea using text-based evidence, clear and convincing reasoning, and/or description.	The response demonstrates coherence and clarity, a logical organization that includes an introduction and conclusion, and a logical progression of ideas.	The response establishes and maintains an effective style, including precise language, descriptive words and phrases, connecting words and phrases, and academic vocabulary.	The response demonstrates a command of standard English conventions consistent with effectively edited writing.
3	The response addresses the prompt and shows effective development of the topic using text-based evidence, reasoning, and/or description.	The response demonstrates some logical organization and includes an introduction and conclusion	Some descriptive words, as well as some connecting words and phrases, are used to express ideas with clarity.	The response demonstrates a command of standard English conventions, although there may be some minor errors in grammar and usage.
2	The response addresses the prompt and shows some development of the topic but fails to use text-based evidence, reasoning, and/or description.	The response demonstrates little logical organization and includes either an introduction or a conclusion.	Few descriptive words, as well as a few connecting words and phrases, are used and ideas are not expressed as clearly as possible.	The response demonstrates a command of standard English conventions, although there are major errors in grammar and usage.

	Development of Ideas	Organization	Clarity of Language	Language and Conventions
1	The response does not directly address the prompt, shows no development of the topic, and fails to use text-based evidence, reasoning and/or description.	The response demonstrates little logical organization and fails to include either an introduction or a conclusion.	No descriptive words or connecting words or phrases are used and ideas are not expressed with clarity.	Errors in grammar and usage create confusion of meaning.
0	The response demonstrates no evidence of the ability to write a response to literature.			

TASK 4 NARRATIVE

Page 179

1. b.

2. Prose Constructed-Response

Scoring Notes: Use the rubric to evaluate student responses. Responses may include but are not include but are not limited to:

- Evidence that Athens, Greece has a sunny and warm climate, situated relatively close to the beach.

- Evidence that Athens, Georgia has a pleasant climate. As it is located in a south Atlantic state, students may also understand that Athens, Georgia is warm and humid most of the year, with mild winters.

2	The response gives sufficient evidence of the ability to utilize factual information from multiple sources to support a narrative.
1	The response gives limited evidence of the ability to utilize factual information from multiple sources to support a narrative.
0	The response gives no evidence of the ability to support a narrative with factual information from multiple sources.

3. Prose Constructed-Response

Scoring Notes: Use the rubric to evaluate student responses. Responses may include but are not include but are not limited to:

- Evidence that a visitor would be able to go to the beach in Athens, Greece.

- Evidence that a visitor would be able to walk a nature trail in Athens, Georgia.

- Evidence that a visitor would be able to spend more time outside in Athens, Greece, because of the amount of sunshine it gets.

- Evidence that a visitor would be able to attend concerts and hear great music in Athens, Georgia.

2	The response gives sufficient evidence of the ability to utilize factual information from multiple sources to support a narrative.
1	The response gives limited evidence of the ability to utilize factual information from multiple sources to support a narrative.
0	The response gives no evidence of the ability to support a narrative with factual information from multiple sources.

Page 180
Narrative

Scoring Notes: Use the rubric to evaluate student responses.

	Development of Ideas	Organization	Clarity of Language	Language and Conventions
4	The response addresses the prompt and effectively establishes a narrator, setting, and characters.	The response demonstrates coherence and clarity, a logical organization that includes an introduction and conclusion, and a logical progression of ideas.	The response establishes and maintains an effective style, including precise language, descriptive words and phrases, connecting words and phrases, and dialogue.	The response demonstrates a command of standard English conventions consistent with effectively edited writing.

	Development of Ideas	Organization	Clarity of Language	Language and Conventions
3	The response addresses the prompt and adequately establishes a narrator, setting, and characters.	The response demonstrates some logical organization and includes an introduction and conclusion.	Some descriptive words, as well as some connecting words and phrases, are used to express ideas with clarity.	The response demonstrates a command of standard English conventions, although there may be some minor errors in grammar and usage.
2	The response addresses the prompt, but inconsistently establishes a narrator, setting, and characters.	The response demonstrates little logical organization and includes either an introduction or a conclusion.	Few descriptive words and few connecting words and phrases are used, and ideas are not expressed as clearly as possible.	The response demonstrates a command of standard English conventions, although there are major errors in grammar and usage.
1	The response does not directly address the , but inconsistently establishes a narrator, setting, and characters.	The response demonstrates little logical organization and fails to include either an introduction or a conclusion.	No descriptive words or connecting words and phrases are used, and ideas are not expressed with clarity.	Errors in grammar and usage create confusion of meaning.
0	The response demonstrates no evidence of the ability to write a narrative.			